SWEET LUNACY

Divine Intoxication in Sufi Lore

OTHER RENDITIONS BY VRAJE ABRAMIAN
FOR HOHM PRESS

NOBODY SON OF NOBODY
Poems of Shaikh Abu-Saeed Abil-Kheir

THIS HEAVENLY WINE
Poems from the Divan-e Jami

SWEET SORROWS
Selected Poems of Sheikh Farideddin Attar Neyshaboori

THE SOUL AND A LOAF OF BREAD
The Teachings of Sheikh Abol-Hasan of Kharaqan

WINDS OF GRACE
Poetry, Stories and Teachings of Sufi Mystics and Saints

SWEET LUNACY

Divine Intoxication in Sufi Lore

Renditions by Vraje Abramian

Hohm Press
Chino Valley, Arizona

Cover Design: Kubera Book Design, Prescott, Arizona

Interior Design and Layout: Kubera Book Design, Prescott, Arizona

Library of Congress Cataloging-in-Publication Data

Names: Abramian, Vraje, translator compiler.
Title: Sweet lunacy : divine intoxication in Sufi lore / renditions
   by Vraje Abramian.
Description: Chino Valley, Arizona : Hohm Press, 2020. | Includes
bibliographical references. | Summary: The translator has selected a
variety of poems and stories from the Islamic Sufi tradition each of
which refer to a type of «divine intoxication.» He has translated them
from the original Farsi. Divine intoxication is a state of absorption
in the One, the Beloved, sometimes characterized by madness or
unconventional behavior, and generally with a tone of longing.--
Provided by publisher.
Identifiers: LCCN 2019055951 (print) | LCCN 2019055952 (ebook) |
ISBN 9781942493570 (paperback) | ISBN 9781942493594 (ebook)
Subjects: LCSH: Sufi poetry, Persian--Translations into English. |
Persian poetry--Translations into English.
Classification: LCC PK6449.E5 S94 2020 (print) | LCC PK6449.E5
(ebook) | DDC 297.4/382--dc23
LC record available at https://lccn.loc.gov/2019055951
LC ebook record available at https://lccn.loc.gov/2019055952

Hohm Press
P.O. Box 4410
Chino Valley, AZ 86323
800-381-2700
http://www.hohmpress.com

This book was printed in the U.S.A. on recycled, acid-free paper using
soy ink.

Humbly dedicated to Huzur

and to the present Master, Baba Ji.

⌒

If reason could understand
how happy my heart is
chained to Your curls
the wise would surrender their sanity
and run after my chains[1]

Ha'fez

⌒

A bird flies in the skies above
while its shadow on the ground
seems to run

A fool becomes a hunter after the shadow
chasing a phantom wasting this precious time

But should one have the shadow of God on earth
as his protector and guide
from illusions and phantoms he is protected
for such a one
dead to the world and alive in God
is God's true servant[2]

Rumi, *Masnavi*

CONTENTS

CONTENTS

I

The Story of This Book

In his or her heart of hearts, every human being nurses a nostalgia remote and nameless, a longing for something one cannot express and should one try to, even farther into the background it recedes. Most of us get on with "the business of life" and learn to have fewer and fewer reasons for such thoughts.

But some amongst us are not so "well adjusted." To these, the business of life is to pursue this mystery, which, in the interest of conformity, the adult human is encouraged to forfeit. By whatever name one may call them, eccentrics, misfits, lunatics, wise fools or saints, they are destined to sink beneath or rise above the conventional wisdom of their time and place, and march to the beat of a different drum.

This book, then, is about those who, for reasons which might not seem altogether reasonable to our everyday mind and logic, question this mystery called life and, unwilling to accept readymade answers and hearsay, seek to find their own through that most individual of struggles which many may choose to avoid.

Jesus said,
> Show me the stone that the builders have
> rejected: that is the cornerstone.[3]
> *Gospel According to Thomas*

Only an idiot and a genius break man-made
laws and they are the nearest to the heart of God.[4]
Kahlil Gibran

Life is made of limits, but understanding is limitless. Using the limited to approach the limitless that's dangerous. To do this and consider it understanding—that's extremely dangerous.[5]

Chuang Tzu

II

Conventions and Questions

We have our discursive (versus transcendental) mind to manage
our individual and community affairs to ensure survival. However,
we may each conceive our existence and its purpose differently.
This is Rumi's version—

> Like a piece of straw
> under which is hidden an ocean
> our body is a cover
> which conceals us in this world.
> Tell me now—how can a piece of straw hide the ocean beneath?
> How can a handful of mud cover this sun?[6]
>   Rumi, *Masnavi*

The human is a mystery. Angels and demons are said to be
unwilling to tread where humans commute, for humans have the
blessing/curse of being able to choose between good and evil. More
than anything else, it is perhaps this quality that makes the human
experience as rewarding as it is daunting, for it is in this precarious
position that we have the potential to find our way to the Mystery
entrusted to us, the Unity which neither the angels nor the demons
were meant to comprehend, the Oneness which multiplicity hints
at, while concealing it at the same time.

> The privilege of few—
> Eternity—obtained—in Time
> Reversed Divinity—

That our ignoble Eyes
The quality conceive
Of Paradise superlative—
Through their comparative.[7]

Emily Dickinson

Once this urge gains the necessary momentum, it abandons conventional wisdom in favor of that uncharted, inner domain which can be traversed by no one but the individual him or herself obeying what, for lack of a better word, may be called intuition. Bodhidharma,* the Buddhist Sage who brought Buddhism to China is quoted saying:

True merit consists in the subtle comprehension
    of pure wisdom
whose substance is silent and void. But this kind
    of merit cannot be
pursued according to the ways of the world.[8]

Those who embark on this search in earnest have to move beyond popular wisdom and pursue that which may make no sense to the mainstream—

Wisdom's mandate
is binding to a sober heart

One lost to this lunacy
is exempt from all such plight[9]

Sheikh Kamal Khojandi

Such characters often disdain the public eye and live lives of obscurity, though some may, in retrospect, gain world renown

---

* Bodhidharma was by some accounts a "Persian monk, who arrived in China around 480..." *The Golden Age of Zen*, John C. Wu, p. 34. (Biblio)

and change human history. Names like John the Baptist, Jesus of Nazareth, Shams of Tabriz and Siddhartha Gautama (Buddha) come to mind readily.

Old Days and These Days

In his introduction to *Holy Madness*, George Feuerstein says—

> Holy fools became rare in the seventeenth century and, with the dawning of the Age of Reason, all but vanished along with saints and mystics. This was, in the words of French historian Michael Foucault, the time of the "great confinement" in an economically troubled Europe... The foundations for the work ethos and the spiritual impoverishment of our own era had been laid.[10]

Thus, we became "rational" beings and whatever did not appeal to our Cartesian, discursive mind became suspect. In time, "I think, therefore I am" (rather than something to the effect of "What amazing wonder that one can not only be, but actually ponder being") facilitates a state of affairs wherein an obese ego (therefore a famished spirit?) becomes the standard.

The spiritually debilitating imbalance that plagues the post-Renaissance human is perhaps best demonstrated by the following anecdote:

> ...a student came to a Rabbi and said, "In the olden days there were men who saw the face of God. Why don't they anymore?"
> The Rabbi replied, "Because nowadays no one can stoop so low."[11]

And yet, perhaps what ails us is not so much a function of place and time trends, but of our misinterpretation of the nature of our basic thirst. Perhaps our breakneck speed in acquiring pleasures and possessions is a misdirected search for happiness and fulfillment.

Happiness and Pleasure

> Adventure most unto itself
> The soul condemned to be—
> Attended by a single Hound
> Its own identity.[12]

Emily Dickinson

Our nostalgia is a memory, however dim, of a state of being which can perhaps best be verbalized as unconditioned (absolute, identity-less) Consciousness.

Once one takes birth, one's memory of the placeless, timeless "above" (our soul) finds itself at the mercy of a body/mind-fabricated identity, which never stops hounding it. The bird that is used to flying the infinite, eternal skies free of all form is now over-ruled and caged in the custom-made dungeon of the individual ego-mind.

The malady from which humans suffer cannot be cured by material, sensual or mental indulgence for these only further burden us until we begin to question in earnest whether happiness and pleasure are the same.

The Business of Life

> The birth of a man is the birth of his sorrow.
> The longer he lives, the more stupid he becomes, because his anxiety to avoid the unavoidable death becomes more and more acute. What bitterness! He lives for what is always out of reach. His thirst for survival in the future makes him incapable of living in the present.[13]

Chuang Tzu

In our ordinary state, each one of us worships that which he or she calls "me," our persona on the stage of existence. This "me" has no real substance, but is a fabrication of the play we find ourselves in. Deep down, we know there is more to this "me" than meets the eye. Meanwhile, we keep witnessing our co-actors in life vanishing without a trace as the play progresses.

Throughout time, sages have said the only way to make sense of our lives is to try to know one's true self. This is not possible by consuming information, hearsay, but only through personal experience. True spirituality aims to release the non-created, self-radiant wisdom that gets buried under the adult human's hopes and fears of tomorrow, delights and regrets of yesterday, and notions of life and death. This process is, therefore, one of unlearning our circumstantial knowledge and ultimately trusting that which cannot be known!

> O' my friend there is a knowledge which is everywhere, which is Atman, which is in me and you and every being... I am beginning to believe that this knowledge has no worse enemy than the desire to know, than learning.[14]

> Siddhartha

> Understanding that abides in the unknowable is realization.[15]

> Chuang Tzu

Vessel in the Water

The 14th-century Indian saint, Kabir, says—

> Vessel in the water
> and water in the vessel
> water whether within or without.

> The vessel breaks
> and waters reemerge.
> This is the essence
> say the devout.[16]

We are vessels filled with individual consciousness (soul, higher mind, jiva), floating in the infinity of unconditioned, Absolute Consciousness. We need to taste, to re–member the Absolute, before this body, which is essential for the experience, runs its course. The sages say that only by tasting Permanence while still alive (dying before dying, being "born again," dying to the lower self) may a mind/body, tumbling down the slippery slope of uncertainty with only the promise of death as its final destination, hope to find Peace.

> Impermanence exposed reveals eternity
> lay down your bag of skin
> leap on the vehicle supreme.
> This is the song of the Skin Bag
> hearken to it, friends.[17]

> Xu Yun
> 19th-century Chinese Chan (Zen) Master

Logic, Reason and Dying While Living

Our logic has its foundation in what our five incomplete and limited senses can decode and transmit, a severe limitation and a formidable obstacle when one intends to contemplate what may lie beyond.

> An authentic Spirituality is a great reversal of ordinary values.[18]
> George Feuerstein

All genuine spiritual traditions aim at reversing attention from flowing out into the world to turning within and experiencing an inner state where one witnesses Being in the absence of one's "me," tastes Consciousness without being conscious of one's identity, or remembers "one's face before one was born." As we can see, words begin to lose color here, for it is counter-intuitive to try to put into words that Silence where "me" is absent (cessation of not only sound but all mental activity and noise).

Neither can anyone facilitate or offer this experience to anyone else, unless one is what in spiritual traditions is known as a Perfect Master—a mystery whose presence has to be experienced and not speculated about. The key word here, especially for our age of information, is experience, not to be mistaken for information. For only a fool will read or hear about the ocean and assume that he or she knows what swimming in water feels like, whereas all the books written in our entire history on the subject would obviously sound so much blabber to one who takes a dip in the ocean.

What do you have to do?

Pack your bags,
Go to the station without them,
Catch the train,
And leave yourself behind.

Quite so: the only practice—and once.[19]

Wei Wu Wei

Once we experience dying before dying, Masters say we gain our humor back, as it were, and we go through this valley of tears with some measure of equanimity, and perhaps rather than concocting tragicomic schemes to avoid or forget death, we might be able to assign death its due place in our temporary existence.

The Panic-Stricken Salt-doll in the River of Time

Every single one of us is busy 24/7 worshiping a notion called "me," which is no more than a salt-doll in the river of time dissolving as we speak, read, or write.

It is only through denying this destabilizing, undeniable reality that we are able to continue in apparent oblivion from one generation to the next. The purpose of our fast cars, every manner of excess, and all our gross material exaggerations, is to distract ourselves in order perchance to nullify our intrinsic awareness of the insubstantiality of this "me" idea, until the salt doll disappears into the river of time and we miss our chance to attend to the real matter, that of attaining our highest potential in the short span of the average human life.

It is inevitable that once one begins to suspect that there is more to this existence than meets the eye, one has embarked on a journey of self-discovery, a journey which is unique, since every one of us is unique, and therefore our mainstream wisdom, our formal education have little to offer here. In our cherubic times, such quests are considered a mid-life crisis, or a sign of the individual's ill-adjustment, but as Krishnamurti puts it:

> It is no measure of one's health to be well adjusted
> to a profoundly sick society.[20]

We need to experience that which gives meaning to our existence, as princes or paupers and everything in between, and enables us to make sense of ourselves in this domain of constant change. Creature comforts cannot be the answer. If anything, statistics indicate higher suicide rates, substance abuse, and crime in societies with higher living standards. And should we make it to the technocrats' promised land, the industrial utopia where machines and robots with artificial intelligence will provide for our every human need so we may live a leisurely life, the issue of providing meaning to our existence will become only more critical, for our age old objectives of survival and prosperity may thus become less relevant.

The main obstacle to overcome is, of course, our own mind. But only one who has not tried would approach the idea of altering the principles by which we all more or less live, i.e. obeying the dictates of the ego, lightly. This affair is depicted by St. George slaying the Dragon in Christian mysticism, while in Islam it is referred to as *jihad al-akbar*, The Grand Battle. It is through this seemingly impossible undertaking, through surrendering one's claim to one's very identity (ego) that we stand a chance to taste the Ultimate, the Treasure hidden within.

Should this sound like a great contradiction, you are probably right. And that is a great start!

The Sufis and the Wise Lunatics

In the cultures spread from Anatolia and the Caucasus to Kashgar in western China, those who abandon the known in search of the Unknown are called by many names, such as *a'shooqh* in Armenian, *a'sheq* in Persian(Farsi), *a'shikh* in Turkish, mast, rend, darveesh, qalandar, faqir (fakir), *mastana*, *majzoob*, baul, etc. Some in the brotherhood of these itinerant beggars, troubadours, bards, poets, and humorists become well-known characters whose factual or fictional words and exploits become legends coloring the popular culture for generations. Sufi Masters often utilize anecdotes and stories based on such individuals' lives, words, deeds, and their divinely inspired nonconformity within their works and teachings to inspire seekers to struggle against socially sanctioned blindness.

In this collection, a number of such pieces by a few luminaries, rendered into English from original Farsi sources, are offered with the express hope of encouraging the reader to question the sanity of our conventional thinking before doubting the inner urge to uncover the Secret we carry within, and to remember that one whose attachment is to the straw of one's "me" stands to lose the Gift hidden in the depths of the ocean concealed beneath.

Gracious company, we are gathered here

to chart our way to the placeless Place

in search of The One

of Whom one can find no trace,

and to strive to put in words That which no words can express!

Pray, mind not our delusional folly,

and be forgiving of any accidental pretensions to success.

Mind

⌣

The Obstacle

Whoever is granted nearness to You
is called mad.
Whoever is concerned with himself becomes
a stranger to You.[†]

Khaje Abdollah Ansari,
the Pir (Master) of Herat

⌣

Knowledge that does not redeem
you from yourself
is many times worse than ignorance.[‡]

Sanai

[†]   Khaje Abdollah Ansari, GPT, p. 71

[‡]   Divan of Sanai, referenced in *Essays of Elahi-Qomshei*, p. 229

Mind

1.   Beyond both worlds
there exists a Tavern
next to whose truth
this world and the next
are but a dream.

Behold how, drunken on its Wine's dregs
this entire universe
is turning, rushing about madly.

Do not bring your mind into This
for the entire knowledge this world contains
like a donkey caught in quicksand
gets stuck and drowns Here.

And should you ask me about this Mystery
I would have no response other than silence.

Attar

2.   Before your life comes to naught
      seek that knowledge
      that disentangles this knot.

      Leave this nothingness
      that here seems like existence
      and reach for that Being
      which here seems nothingness.

                          Shams of Tabriz

3. How bewildering that to your own light
you remain blind, while in both worlds
every particle wishes for a thousand eyes
to be dazzled by your glorious light.

Attar

4.   Knowing is of two kinds: One is acquired at schools
where through texts and discourse
your intellect may surpass that of others'
though in the process you become burdened with the
        spoils.

The other is granted by the Almighty
and has its source deep within one's soul.
This knowledge that bubbles up from within one's chest
neither goes stale nor changes colors.

Rumi

5. Intellect is wax-footed
    and this Path is red hot.

    Only God knows this
    and the one who has tried.

                    Hosein Elahi-Qomshei

6.   Through this garden one dawn a breeze drifted
      carrying the scent of Your love locks.

      Every rose here still smells
      of this perfumed lunacy.

                              Bee'del of Delhi

7.   Since my mind got a scent of the Wine of Love
it has surrendered its sanity.

How can one who has made his home
in the Lane of Love fit in the two worlds?

Attar

8.   Do not rest assured if a trace is left of your own existence
       for you are still an idol worshipper.

       Suppose some day you abandon this self.
       How will you cure yourself of the illusion
       that you were the one who abandoned yourself
       and cured your illusion?

                    Rumi

9.   The all-knowing heart was Commanded to alight
in this world of harsh faces and hard hearts
like a delicate crystal urn
placed between an anvil and a hammer.

Jami

10.   By God, there is no rascal as clever and sharp
       as the one who quits trickery and cleverness.

       There is no solitude as sublime as that aloofness.

                        Rumi

11.　Reason showed up and began cautioning Lovers.
It blocked the Path and began its clever trickery.

Once it could find no room
in their being for advice and caution
it kissed every Lover's foot
and went to mind its own business.

Rumi

12.   Your journey is beyond this world's.
       You are not of dirt and water.
       You are of something other.

       If your body be the riverbed
       your soul in it is the water of life.

       But where your True Essence lies
       There you have need of neither.

                          Rumi

13.   From the glory of my lunacy
        the entire world has been granted vision.
        Whoever loses all coverings
        is robed in such glorious provision.

Bee'del of Delhi

14.   We seek in enterprise profits not meant for us.
       We beg for alms which cannot be handed to us.

       In schools we search for knowledge they do not possess
       and in cloisters we search for that forbearance
       which they may not need to express.

       God's guile has rendered us blind
       so our soul imagines
       this dungeon called body its rightful home
       clinging to it and remaining fearful
       of the vast open spaces above
       till it is snatched by death and buried in dirt.

                    Rumi

15.   The riddle of love is not within reason's reach.
One does not attempt such delicate matters
by such crude means.

Ha'fez

16.　　Y ou seek your way back to the sea
for you are by nature of the sea.

Ponds, lakes and streams
are to you only limitations.

In the pool of life there is borrowed water only.
No intelligent one should expect permanence here.

Rumi

17.　One of the lunatic sages was asked about *al lateef*, the Delicate One, one of the 99 beautiful names of God, and he said—

Lateef is that which is understood without discussing its howness or whatness.

unknown

18.   The great Sheikh Abu Saeed said—

Whenever they speak of Bu-Saeed everyone feels joy
because from Bu-Saeed's Bu-Saeedness nothing is left.

Sheikh Abu-Saeed

19.   I once heard that one whose heart had vanished
was being tortured by street urchins throwing stones
when of a sudden hail began to drop. Raising his head
the love lunatic said—

    First You steal my heart, then You have me stoned
    and now this hail on my head.
    Have You, too, joined these kids?

               Attar

20.　When I entered the Path of Love
　　　intellect rose declaring in indignation—

　　　　　Those who fall in Love
　　　　　lose all rights to safety and well–being!

　　　　　　　　　　　Sa'di of Shiraz

Heart

⌒

The Battleground

In the human heart
there sits an Essence
which lies outside both worlds.

No one can find of It a trace here
for we have lost Its track.

One who does not
drag reason There by its hair
will learn not a simple word of this Affair. §

Attar

⌒

Unless one's estranged soul
gets a hint of this madness
it may not be cleansed
of its impurities.

My entire Divan
is nothing but the story of this insanity.
Reason is but an alien to this affair.‖

Attar

---

§   Div Attar, p. 248, no. 195, select.

‖   CB, Attar, p. 440, lines 4579–4580

21.   Wherever the world might be headed
where is it that you are headed
and what provisions have you prepared?

If both worlds be filled with idols
what have you chosen as your beloved idol?

Suppose generosity dies and meanness prevails,
my heart and the very light of my eye
where lies your largess and charity?

We squeeze too many words out of our heads
which only deserve to fall on deaf ears.
Enough repeating what others say.
Where are your statements, what is your state?

Rumi

22.   God pulls you to Himself from within
        through a thousand stories
        uttered by no mouth, using no words.
        And should your dumbfounded intellect
        object and demand to know
        how and in what manner, say—

        This happens in a manner which you cannot know,
        and may peace be with you.

                        Rumi

23.   One late night
Leylee whispered thus in Majnoon's heart—

> You who for my sake
> have left reason behind, listen well.
>
> In this love, your sanity you learn to disdain
> for among lovers shrewdness begets only pain.
>
> In the court of love if you wish to fare well
> become a lunatic
> throw your wits to the wind
> plunder your reason
> and from all cleverness abstain.

Attar

24.   O' heart, dance along in this Love.
        O' soul, in agreement offer your head.
        O' patience, flee for you do not possess
        what this Pain takes.
        O' intellect, run along and play
        for in this Affair
        you are no more than a babe born yesterday.

                              Rumi

25.　　O' heart, you became many things
a Sufi, a theologian and a recluse
but you never tried to become a believer
and truly surrender.

Rumi

26.   Beloved, searching for the One who Is
is a drunken affair for one who does not exist.

Reaching for Unity is a sign of insanity
for one who is cast in duality!

                          Khaje Abdollah Ansari

27.   My mind left me a hundred times and again came back
so it would mayhap taste the Wine lovers speak of.

Action and idleness both I have abandoned now
and wonder where all this may finally end up!

Rumi

28.   The day Your Love releases me from sanity
I will relish my joy with such madness
that no demon would ever dare match.

No judge's pen can render unto a convict that
which Your verdict may do to my lovelorn heart.

Rumi

29.   Bayazid, the great mystic, was once asked, "Do you
        know God?"
and he said—

    Is there anyone in the whole world who does not?

Another time when he was lost in the ocean of union and
he was asked the same question, he said—

    Who am I to know God? How could anyone in
    the whole world know God?

                            Khaje Abdollah Ansari

30.   A mad one in the bazaar came across a candy shop.

Dear Sir, he said. Do you have white sugar and almonds?

Lots of both, said the shopkeeper. We shall find out if there be a buyer!

Good Sir, said the lunatic. Why not mix them together and relish the sweet delight? For once you have sold them what can you buy better than them?

Attar

31. Bu-bakr Shebli was once in an expansive mood and he
     said—

>   Beloved Almighty, make everyone blind
>   so no one can see You but me.

Another time when he felt in utter spiritual contraction,
he said—

>   Lord, make Shebli blind so one such as me
>   may not look at Your Beauty.

Khaje Abdollah Ansari

32.   Imam Jafar Sadeq said—

Divine Love is a kind of Lunacy,
It is neither to be blamed nor praised.

Attar

33.   One day, Bohlool, the mad one, went to Haroon's
        palace and for the briefest moment before he could be
        chased away, placed himself on Al-Rasheed's throne!
        Whereupon he was beaten severely till every limb on him
        was black and blue. Bleeding and breathless the lunatic
        addressed the monarch thus—

> I was on the throne but for a breath
> and behold what has come upon me.
> You who will spend a lifetime there
> be wary and be herewith warned
> of what you might invite upon yourself.

                    Attar

34.   "I am the one who is seeking,"
      intellect appeared and thus boasted.

      It had obviously taken leave of its senses.
      I, therefore, had to promptly chasten it and show it its
            place.#

      Vain-footed imagination concocted many roadmaps and
            ways
      but it returned empty-handed from the Beloved's Gate.

      Whoever does not speak of You had better be silent.
      Whatever does not remind one of You is better forgotten.

      Rend all veils, Beloved, and appear in our midst as the
            Oneness of Unity.
      And if I should be the veil, pray tear me asunder.

      We pray in no direction other than Yours.
      Who would take pity on us if You do not favor us?

                              Nezami Ganjavi

In Sufi lore one does not seek unless one is sought (by the Beloved). The
    Sufis find the mind's discursive thinking incapable of fathoming the
    intricacies of the Divine Love Affair.

35.   In a book called *Ajaeb-nameh,* Book of Wonders, there
is a story about Sultan Mahmood Of Qazne which goes
like this:

One day Sultan Mahmood, while chasing game, came
across a lunatic sitting on a bridge who addressed him
and said—

O Mahmood, last night I had a dream. I dreamt that
I was sitting on your throne and Qazne (the capital
city) was mine and Ayaz, your favorite servant, was
standing in attendance.

And then? said an irate Sultan Mahmood.

And then I awoke and saw none of that. You see,
tomorrow you will close your eyes and of your realm,
your treasures and servants you will see no trace.
Then you will realize you and I are of the same cloth!

Attar

36.　Someone was complaining about the world and all in it.
A wise one said—

> This is a comedy, a humorous play in the eyes of the
> elect. But in the eyes of minors it is serious, and a
> place of do's and don'ts. Now if you cannot handle
> this as a humorous affair, do not play. But if you can,
> then be jolly and enjoy it in good humor, for a playful
> game's flavor is enhanced by laughter and mirth and
> by leaving tears out.

Shams of Tabriz

37.   Rabia-addawiya, the lady saint of Basra, was asked how
       she had attained that high station, and she said—

       …by losing all attainments and all stations in the One.

                          Attar

38.   The pious ascetic announced—

One obeys religion through abstention.

The Sheikh theologian, mirror in hand,
pronounced the Path as the way to salvation.

Our lunatic, to the dismay of both
dropped at once all coverings
and nakedly declared—

Witness the ultimate solution!

When one arrives There
where neither the wayfarer nor the way remain
when one's very existence has been offered
then one is said to have attained true poverty.

                    Bee'del of Delhi

39.   Hamdoon Qassar of Neyshaboor said—

The clever are beguiled by their own cleverness.

And he said—

Have this world in contempt and those who run after
it will have you in high regard.

And he said—

Only one who accuses God complains of calamities
and hardships that befall him. The Devil and his
brood rejoice when someone commits murder, when
one dies faithless, and when one's heart is possessed
by fear of poverty.

Attar

40.   A lunatic unable to tell his head from his foot
dejected by everyone's strange attitude
and unable to figure out his own
felt downcast. Lost in his infinite thoughts
he raised his head to his Lord and moaned thus—

O' Knower of every mystery
when this creation's head from its tail
no one seems to be able to tell
how long of this coming and going here?
Does Your heart feel not heavy of creating?

Attar

41.　Someone asked a mad one—

What is pain? For you seem like you would know.

Pain, said the derelict, is when you want something
like a ten-day thirst wants water, and yet you cannot
tell what it is, since for It you have not a name!

Attar

42. A single awakened eye does the work of a hundred
    lanterns.
    From this house of darkness carve out a window into
    your heart.

    Better than erecting palaces that rise up to the heavens
    is in the deserts of insanity to dance like a breeze.

                    Bee'del of Delhi

43.   Reason is like unto a drop separated from the sea.
        What could it contain from Love's oceans?

        Like a tailor, mind stitches many pieces together
        but never can it produce a garment
        worthy of Love's slender height.

                              Attar

44. Tear down the cover that veils your inner meaning
for you don't find your way within
unless you become a destroyer of veils.

Should the entire world come out as your enemy
if you are after this Prize do not turn your back but
remain aware.

Should the entire creation turn into hail and rain upon
your head
reach not for a shield but bear it.

If you be the world's cleverest,
wise you will not be deemed
until to Love you surrender your sanity
and with every breath insist and be more insane.

Attar

45. One who fails to find intimacy with the Beloved here
will forever remain an alien.

Whoever is not stuck in his arrogance
and not ruled by his capricious mind
will not call my words fiction
or say that I am out of my mind.

Attar

Deliverance

⁓

The Journey

The Prophet (peace be upon him) said—

O seeker of mysteries
if you want to behold one who after death lives
search for one who while still alive
has witnessed being in the higher worlds.

Die before you die, He said.

And this mystery one may comprehend
not through intellect
but through dying before one's death.*

Rumi

⁓

By God, no wise one was ever spared
headaches engendered by the vulgar
or heartaches caused by the elite.

Hear and apply this sincere advice—
Become a lunatic
be not wise! †

Khaje Abol-vafa Kharazmi
"Pir-e Fereshte"
(The Angelic Master)

---

* Mas bk 6, p. 1062, lines 8, 11 and 20

† PF, p. 12, no. 39

46. First empty your head, then declare to it—

    O' joyous empty bowl
    be now a goblet to Love's Mystery.

    In Love you have ever had your nest
    O' everlasting bird of eternities.
    Hold on to Love firmly
    forever rest in this Nest.

               Rumi

47.　　Abandon the confinement made of your attributes.
　　　Take refuge in the attribute-less Infinite
　　　for it is the nature of that Ocean
　　　that the old, the decrepit and the stale
　　　who dare to take a dip in It
　　　are revived and rendered young and fresh.

Khaje Abol-vafa Kharazmi
"Pir-e Fereshte"

48.   Your inner Essence rules over fire
while the layers covering It are but food for fire.

The inner meaning of man is that
over which the ruler of hell has no dominion.

Rumi

49.　The Story of the Grieving Woman

A lunatic asked a woman at a grave site
why the tears and the heart-rending mourning.

My eyes are flooded and my heart burns
for the youth lying under this mound is my child,
said the desperate mother.

You are the one in dirt confined.
He is now nothing but pure light.
While in body one's soul is soiled.
Once one dies
one is redeemed from dirt,
said the grace-mad one and moved on.

Attar

50.   You who will surrender the degrading cage of this body
       when preparing to ascend to higher skies
       know that the shirt offered you here
       is fit for slavery only
       and prepare to afterwards receive your robe of honor.

       Trust, O' noble one
       this mortal coil is nothing but a prison house.
       When it begins to crumble, lament not
       for your soul will glide like a ship on the seas
       once released from the anchor of this body.

                    Rumi

51.   At dawn after raising a goblet
and drinking to the tune of harps and drums
I stashed a flask of ruby wine in reason's saddlebag
and bade farewell to it
on its way to the realms beyond existence.

Ha'fez

52.   Let your coverings drop, slip out of this robe,
      nakedness lacks not in glory.

      Persevere in this Lunacy
      mayhap you shall succeed
      and clothe this bubble with the Ocean itself.

                          Bee'del of Delhi

53.   The human heart is a candle
        whose only yearning is to be lit,
        a gaping wound biding its time
        by the Friend's Presence to be filled.

        Learn to endure this burning
        this wounded patience and waiting
        and someday you will witness
        that Love can never be taught
        that It can only be caught.

                            Rumi

54. Of this intellect one needs to become ignorant
and harbor insanity instead.

Whatever offers you a benefit, run away from.
Drink poison and should you be offered
the cup of eternal life, knock it over!

I have tried and tested this crafty mind.
I am taking refuge in lunacy from now on.

Rumi

55.   Khaje Abdollah said—

The Mystics' rewards are three—
The heavenly music, which invites one to the table of
    Love
spread by the Beloved,
the heavenly wine served There, which loosens
one's tongue,
and the Divine vision which steals one's
attributes and leaves one in a state where
every hair turns into an eye to behold that Beauty.

                            Khaje Abdollah Ansari

56. Deep in my soul I hide this Pain
and this Longing for You.

The Sorrow You have granted me
has brought me a world of joy.

I am so jealous of my Secret
that I hide It even from myself.

Attar

57.   Someone told Jesus-of-Mary—

You whose ceiling touches the sun
why do you not have yourself an abode?

Because I have not lost my mind, said Christ.
Whatever cannot accompany one to eternity
best be forgotten for it is not worthy of the human.

Attar

58. One who appears here and is to return There,
     know that one to be a dew drop
     headed back to the sea momentarily.

     Feel not sorry for the lightning
     if it smile for a flash and disappear
     or a dew drop in the ocean fall and vanish.

     The world of senses is made of nothing.
     Strive for gold for what is here is but copper.

     A life in the realm of the senses,
     next to the Eternal is but a moment.

     Whatever that moment be laden with
     be it paradise itself
     I flee from it.

                         Attar

59.   One who had been nursing a long, patient love
       was finally summoned by the beloved and told—

            Come, for tonight's our night.

       The lover somehow lasted
       till he found himself at the gate
       but now a problem out of nowhere appeared in his mind—

            If I knock and announce myself as me
            I might be told to save my love for myself.
            And if I say, "This too is You beloved."
            Then I might hear, "You are free to leave then, no
                 need of you!"
            What am I to do? How do I present myself without
                 me?

       Thus he spent the night, standing at the door, debating
            the issue.

       This story was told to an earnest one and he said—

            A clever logician perhaps, but a lover he was not,
            for like a true man of intellect he changed a hundred
                 ways
            debating his own questions and answers a hundred
                 times.

       Had he been a lover true he would have entered
       long before mind's trickery had had a chance.

                              *

By the time all your doubts have been tallied
all you have achieved are the futile thoughts.

Though for self-preservation they might be proper
lovers are not acquainted with such calculations.
One whose soul is aflame wants nothing but this Fire.

The Day of Reckoning itself is dim
in comparison to the dawn of Love.

Attar

60. Ebrahim Adham, the King of Bokhara, who abandoned
     his throne to later become a Lighthouse for the seekers
     on the Path, said—

     I do not know which one is harder
     suffering the vicissitudes on the Path in anonymity
     or escaping the horrors a venerating public
     wishes to bestow upon the wayfarer
     once he is discovered.

No one knows where Ebrahim died or where he is buried.

     Attar

61.   Whatever comes into being and is named
is a dream-drop from the ocean of Being.
When that which you call reason you abandon
you will comprehend this inner reality.

One who starts with intellect ends in bewilderment.
True knowledge points the seeker There
where knowledge is revealed to the seeker as ignorance.

Attar

62.   The Meeting of the Seeker and the Soul (Selected from the final episode in "The Seeker's Journey," in Attar's *Moseebat-nameh, The Book of Travails*).

The seeker finally came to the soul and said—

> You who are a ray of the Eternal Sun of Glory
> whatever is in the Absolute is in truth trusted in you.
> One can neither describe you nor assign you
>   attributes
> for you are far beyond intellect and wisdom.
>
> Higher than you nothing is created
> besides you no other is to be loved.
>
> If I am allowed in this life to fathom your grandeur
> I shall reach and reside in Eternal Heights.

⌣

> A hundred worlds you journeyed,
> whispered the soul,
> before you reached this shore.
>
> That which you have lost, if you ever lost It
> resides in you but your being veils It.
> One does not find It till one journeys within.
>
> In this creation you sift the entire world back and
>   forth
> forever asking how, why and wherefrom
> yet you find no one and nothing of worth.

But if the drop should taste the ocean once
all hows, whys and whats without a trace vanish.

The soul offered these thoughts to the seeking mind
as nourishment for the journey ahead
and finding the seeker ready
allowed him a taste of the depths.

When the Pir heard the seeker's tale, he whispered his
blessings—

For as long as you still imagined a self
from the Obvious Mystery
you were obviously veiled.

Not a particle of doubt remains now.
There is no more to gain
Nothing more to do but to vanish from yourself
and vanish yet again.

Now you may begin your Journey.
And you'd do well to *always* remember
that this seeking
is by and from the Friend
for the Friend.

Attar

ABBREVIATIONS

In Citations and Footnotes

AN: Kadkani, Dr. Mohammad Reza Shafiee, editor. *Asrar-Nameh* [The Book of Mysteries] by Sheikh Farideddin Attar Neyshaboori. From the Attar Collection, no. 4, 1st Edition. Tehran: Sokhan Publications, 2007.

Aref.: Masoomi, Reza. *Arefaneha, Jami az Oqianoos-e Beekaran-e Erfan* [Selections of Mystic Poetry, A Cup From the Infinite Ocean of Gnosi]. 6th Edition. Original Farsi. Khayyam Collection: p. 198-258. Tehran. Nashr-e Eshare Publications, 1991.

BPM: Kadkani, Dr. Mohammad Reza Shafiee, editor. *Bee'del Dehlavi, Sha'er-e Aieeneha [Bee'del of Delhi, the Poet of Mirrors], A Study of Persian Poetry Produced in the Indian Subcontinent.* 6th Edition. Tehran: Agah Publications, 2005 (1384AH).

BWS: Kadkani, Dr. Mohammad Reza Shafiee, editor. *An Sooy-e Harf va Sout* [Beyond Words and Sound]. From the Farsi Literary Heritage Series. Selected pieces from Asrarottohid (of Sheikh Abu-Saeed Abil Kheir). 3rd Edition. Tehran: Sokhan Publications, 2009 (1388AH).

CB: Kadkani, Dr. Mohammad Reza Shafiee, editor. *Mateq-attair* [Conference of the Birds]. 11th Edition. From the Attar Collection, No. 1. Tehran: Sokhan Publications, 2012 (1391AH).

Div. Att.: Mansoor, Jahangeer, editor. *Divan of Attar* by Sheikh Farideddin Attar Neyshaboori. Biography by Badiozzaman Foroozanfar. 5th Edition. Tehran: Sokhan Publications, 2006.

Div J.: Jami, aka Nur al-Din Abdal-Rahman ibd Ahmad Jami. *Divan-e Jami. Vol. I: Fatehat al-shabab, Vol. II: Wasetat al-aqd and Khatemat al-hayat.* Edited by Ala Khan Afsahzad. Tehran: Written Heritage Publication Office, Center for Iranian Studies, 1999.

Div. Sh.: Jalal al-Din Rumi, Maulana. *Kolliyat-e Shams-e Tabrizi; Divan-e ghazali-yat* [The Complete Divan of Shams of Tabriz]. Intro and essay on Rumi's biography by Badiozzaman Foroozanfar. Tehran: Muasseseye, Matbuatiye Amir Kabir, Amir Kabir Publications, 1958.

EN: Kadkani, Dr. Mohammad Reza Shafiee, editor. *Elahee-nameh* [The Book of the Beloved] by Sheikh Farideddin Attar Neyshaboori. From the Attar Collection, No. 2. Tehran: Sokhan Publications, 2006.

EQ: Elahi-Qomshei, Hosein. *Maq-alat,* [Essays]. 10th Edition. Tehran: Leyla Publications, 2003 (1382AH).

FR: Ahmadi, Babak. *Chahar Gozaresh az Tazkerat ol-Owliya-e 'Attar,* [Four Reports, Studies of Tazkarat-ol Olya (Biography of the Saints) by Shayk Fariduddin Attar]. First Edition. Tehran: Nashr-e Markaz, 1997.

GL: Gazargahi, aka Hosein Shahabeddin Esmeel Tabasi Heravi. *Majalis-ol-Oshshaq, Tazkar-e Orafa,* [Gatherings of Lovers, Biographies of Mystics]. Edited by Qhikam Reza Tabatabaie Majd. 2nd Edition. Tehran: Zarrin Publications, 1996.

GPT: Ansari of Herat, Khaje Abdollah, editor. *Goftar-e Pir-e Tariqat* [The Sayings of the Master of the Path] by Saber Kermani. 8th Edition. Tehran: Eqbal Publishers, 2002 (1381AH).

Haf: Bakhtiari, Hosein Pejhman, editor. *Divan-e Kamel-e Ha'fez-e Shirazi* [The Complete Divan of Khaje Ha'fez of Shiraz]. First Edition. Tehran: Forooqi Publications, 1997.

Maq-Mov: Movahhed, Mohammad Ali, editor. *Maqalat-e Shams-e Tabrizi, Shamseddin Mohammad Tabrizi* [The Essays of Shams of Tabriz]. 3rd Edition. Tehran: Kharazami Publications, 2006 (1385AH).

Mas: Darvish, M., editor. *Masnavi-e Manavi Molavi.* Version according to K. Nicholson. Preface and biography by Professor Badiozzaman Foroozanfar. 10ᵗʰ Edition. Tehran: Javidan Publications, 1996.

MKN: Kadkani, Dr. Mohammad Reza Shafiee, editor. *Mokhtarnameh* [The Book of the Sovereign, Attar's Rubais] by Sheikh Farideddin Attar Neyshaboori. First Edition. From the Attar Collection, No. 3. Tehran: Sokhan Publications, 2007.

MN: Kadkani, Dr. Mohammad Reza Shafiee, editor. *Moseebatnameh* [The Book of Travails] by Sheikh Farideddin Attar Neyshaboori. First Edition. From the Attar Collection, No. 3. Tehran: Sokhan Publications, 2007.

NB: Kadkani, Dr. Mohammad Reza Shafiee, editor. *Neveshtebar-darya, az miras-e erfani-e Sheikh Abol-Hasan-e Kharaqani* [Scripture on the Sea, from the Spiritual Legacy of Sheikh Abol-Hasan of Kharaqan]. Tehran: Sokhan Publications, 1988.

PF: Shirazi, Seyyed Ahmad Beheshti, editor. *The Rubais of Khaje Abol-vafa Kharazmi, known as Pir-e Freshte (The Angelic Master).* First Edition. Tehran: Rozaneh Publications, 2016 (1395AH).

PG: Ayati, Abdol-Mohammad, editor. *Makhzan-ol-asrar* [Container of Secrets, from "Panj-Ganj," Five Treasures] by Nizami Ganjavi. Second Edition. Tehran: Islamic Revolution Publications, 1991.

PSD: Kadkani, Dr. Mohammad Reza Shafiee. *Zaban-e She'r dar Nasr-e Sufieh* [Poetry in Sufi Discourse, an Introduction to Elements of Style in Mystic Expression]. From the Iranian Mystic Heritage, Meeras-e Erfani-e Iran Series. Tehran: Sokhan Publications, 2013.

QM-1 (Vol.1) and QM-2 (Vol.2): Ansari, Khaje Abdollah. *Tafsir-e Adabi va 'Erfani-ye Quran-e Majid* [Literal and Mystic Interpretation of the Holy Qor'an]. Ahmad Meiybodi, editor. Two volumes in Farsi. 17ᵗʰ Edition. Tehran: Eqbal Publications, 2005.

S.Sh.: Foroughi, Mohammad Ali. *Kolleeyyat-e Sa'di-e Shirazi, Golestan, Boostan, Qazaleeyyat, Qasaed, Robaeeyyat, Qata'at* [Complete Works of Sa'di including Golestan, Boostan, Gazals]. 3ʳᵈ Edition. Tehran: Negah Publications, 1991 (1375AH).

SEP: Vafaie, Mohammad Afsheen, editor. *Resaleye Sephahsalar dar Manaqeb-e Hazrat Khodavandgar* [Sepahsalar's Essay on Rumi] by Fereydoon ebn-e Ahmad Sepahsalar]. Tehran: Sokhan Publications, 2006 (1385).

ST: Kadkani, Dr. Mohammad Reza Shafiee, editor. *Chesheedan-e Ta'm-e Vaqt,* [Savoring the Taste of Time: Old and New Statements of Sheikh Abu-Saeed]. From the Iranian Spiritual Heritage Series, No. 3: The Mystic Heritage of Abu-Saeed Abil-Kheir, First Edition. Tehran: Sokhan Publications, 2006.

TAZ: Attar, Farid ad-Din. *Tazkerat-al-owlia* [Memorial of the Saints] Edited by Mohammad Este'lami. 8th Edition. Tehran: Zavvar Publications, 1995 (1374AH).

CITATIONS
See *ABBREVIATIONS* or *BIBLIOGRAPHY* for full citation

Front Matter

no. 1 – Haf p. 159, no. 11

no. 2 – Mas bk 1, p. 417

no. 3 – Ehrman, "The Gospel According to Thomas," *The Other Gospels: Accounts of Jesus From Outside the New Testament.*

no. 4 – Gibran, *Sand and Foam*, p. 21

no. 5 – Chuang Tzu, *Inner Chapters*, p. 33

no. 6 – Mas bk 4, pp. 675-676

no. 7 – Dickenson, *The Complete Poems of Emily Dickenson*, p. 390, no. 800

no. 8 – Wu, *The Golden Age of Zen*, p. 35

no. 9 – GL, p. 213

no. 10 – Feuerstein, *Holy Madness*, p. 19

no. 11 – Cheetham, *Green Man, Earth Angel*, p. 61, Ref to C. G. Jung, *Memories, Dreams and Reflections.*

no. 12 – Dickenson, *The Complete Poems of Emily Dickenson*, p. 399, no. 822

no. 13 – Chuang Tzu, as quoted in *The Tibetan Book of Living and Dying*, p. 17

no. 14 – Hesse, *Siddhartha.* p. 11

no. 15 – Chuang Tzu, *Inner Chapters*, p. 28

no. 16 – Kabir, "Songs of the Heart" *Poetry of Kabir*

no. 17 – Xu Yun, "The Song of the Skin Bag," *Empty Cloud, The Autobiography of the Chinese Zen Master Xu Yun.* pp. 214–217

no. 18 – Feuerstein, *Holy Madness* p. 21

no. 19 – Wei Wu Wei, *Open Secret*

no. 20 – *Samadhi*, Awakentheworldfilm

Poems and Stories
Part One: Mind, The Battleground
1. Div. Att. p. 158, no. 37, lines 4, 6, 8, & 10
2. Div. Sh. p. 1320, no. 106
3. Div. Att. p. 159, no. 38, lines 11, 12, 13, 14, 25 & 26
4. Mas bk 4, pp. 1964–5, lines 1960, 1962, 1964, 1965
5. EQ p. 298
6. BPM p. 141, no. 37, lines 3 & 4
7. Div. Att. pp. 180–181, no. 75, selected
8. Div. Sh. p. 1334, no. 260
9. Div. J. bk 1, p. 65, no. 269
10. Div. Sh. p. 1325, no. 152
11. Div. Sh. p. 1344, no. 367
12. Div. Sh. p. 1478, no. 1821
13. BPM p. 170, no. 77 (entire piece)
14. Mas bk 6, p. 1090, lines 6, 8, 22, 23, and 24
15. Haf p. 213, no. 105
16. Div. Sh. p. 1280, no. 3436
17. PSD p. 75
18. ST p. 126, no. 3
19. AN p. 181
20. S. Sh. p. 422, ta.50, line 1

Part Two: Heart, The Battleground
21. Div. Sh. p. 804, no. 2144
22. Mas bk 6, p.1076, lines 20 and 23
23. Div. Att. p. 180, no. 74
24. Div. Sh. p. 1440, no. 1406
25. Div. Sh. p. 1470, no. 1731
26. PSD p. 397
27. Div. Sh. p. 1379, no. 752
28. Div. Sh. p. 1376, no. 720
29. QM-2 p. 372
30. AN p. 228
31. QM-2 p. 385
32. TAZ p. 7

33. MN p. 213, no. 1017
34. PG p. 3, no. 20; p. 2, no. 19; pp. 28, 29; p. 7, no. 63
35. EN p. 653, 654, no. 4350
36. Maq-Mov pp. 312, 313
37. TAZ p. 79
38. BPM p. 309
39. TAZ pp. 403 and 404
40. EN p. 453, no. 12
41. EN p. 390, no.3
42. BPM p. 174, no. 83, lines 7, 8, 9 and 10
43. Div. Att. p. 405, no. 449, lines 3–6
44. Div. Att. p. 576, no. 761, lines 3, 4, 5, and 8
45. Div. Att. p. 567, no. 745, lines 3, 4 and 5

Part Three: Deliverance, The Journey
46. Div. Sh. p. 488, no. 1248
47. PF p. 11
48. Div. Sh. p. 1220, no. 3297
49. MN p. 191, no. 8/4
50. Div. Sh. p. 1220, no. 3297
51. Haf p. 383, no. 429, selected
52. BPM p. 326
53. Div. Sh. p. 1485, no. 1900
54. Mas bk 2, lines 2328–29 and 2332
55. QM-2 p. 574
56. MKN p. 113, no. 309
57. MN p. 413, no. 10/36
58. MN p. 413, line 6358–6362
59. MN p. 431, no. 1/39, selected
60. TAZ p. 111
61. MN p. 445, lines 7062–7079
62. MN pp. 437–442, selected

BIBLIOGRAPHY

Ahmadi, Babak. *Chahar Gozaresh az Tazkerat ol-Owliya-e 'Attar,* [Four Reports, Studies of Tazkarat-ol Olya (Biography of the Saints) by Shaykh Fariduddin Attar]. First Edition. Tehran: Nashr-e Markaz, 1997.

Ansari of Herat, Khaje Abdollah. *Goftar-e Pir-e Tariqat* [The Sayings of the Master of the Path]. Edited by Saber Kermani. 8th Edition. Tehran: Eqbal Publishers, 2002 (1381AH).

Ansari, Khaje Abdollah. *Tafsir-e Adabi va 'Erfani-ye Quran-e Majid* [Literal and Mystic Interpretation of the Holy Qor'an]. Edited by Ahmad Meiybodi. 17th Edition. Tehran: Eqbal Publications, 2005.

Attar, Farid ad-Din. *Tazkerat-al-owlia* [Memorial of the Saints]. Edited by Mohammad Este'lami. 8th Edition. Tehran: Zavvar Publications, 1995 (1374AH).

Ayati, Abdol-Mohammad, editor. *Makhzan-ol-asrar* [Container of Secrets, from "Panj-Ganj," Five Treasures] by Nizami Ganjavi. Second Edition. Tehran: Islamic Revolution Publications, 1991.

Bakhtiari, Hosein Pejhman, editor. *Divan-e Kamel-e Hafez-e Shirazi* [The Complete Divan of Khaje Ha'fez of Shiraz]. First Edition. Tehran: Forooqi Publications, 1997.

Cheetham, Tom. *Green Man, Earth Angel: The Prophetic Tradition and the Battle for the Soul of the World.* SUNY Series in Western Esoteric Traditions. Albany, NY: SUNY Publications, State University of New York Press, 2005.

Darvish, M., editor. *Masnavi-e Manavi Molavi*. Version according to K. Nicholson. Preface and biography by Professor Badiozzaman Foroozanfar. 10th Edition. Tehran: Javidan Publications, 1996.

Dickenson, Emily. *The Complete Poems of Emily Dickenson*. Edited by Thomas H. Johnson. First Paperback Edition. Boston and New York: Little, Brown and Company, 1961.

Elahi-Qomshei, Hosein. *Maq-alat, Essays*. 10th Edition. Tehran: Leyla Publications, 2003 (1382AH).

Ehrman, Bartram, editor and Zlatko Plese, trans. And eds. *The Other Gospels: Accounts of Jesus from Outside the New Testament*. New York: Oxford University Press, 2014.

Esfahani, Seyyed Ahmad Hatef. *Divan-e Hatef-e Esfahani* [Divan of Hatef of Esfahan]. Edited by Vaheed Dastgerdi. Biography by Eqbal Ashtiani. Second Edition. Tehran: Negah Publications, 1991 (1374AH).

Feuerstein, Georg. *Holy Madness, Spirituality, Crazy-Wise Teachers, and Enlightenment*. Prescott, Arizona: Hohm Press, 2006.

Foroughi, Mohammad Ali. *Kolleeyyat-e Sa'di-e Shirazi, Golestan, Boostan, Qazaleeyyat, Qasaed, Robaeeyyat, Qata'at* [Complete Works of Sa'di including Golestan, Boostan, Gazals]. 3rd Edition. Tehran: Negah Publications, 1991 (1375AH).

Gazargahi, aka Hosein Shahabeddin Esmeel Tabasi Heravi. *Majalis-ol-OShshaq, Tazkar-e Orafa* [Gatherings of the Lovers, Biographies of Mystics]. Edited by Qhikam Reza Tabatabaie Majd. 2nd Edition. Tehran: Zarrin Publications, 1996.

Gibran, Khalil. *Sand and Foam*. Edited by Will Johnson. New York: Alfred A. Knopf, 1995.

Hinton, David, translator. *Chuang-Tzu: The Inner Chapters*. Washington D.C.: Counterpoint, 1997.

Hesse, Hermann. *Siddhartha*. Dover Thrift Editions. New York: Dover Publications, 1999.

Jami, aka Nur al-Din Abdal-Rahman ibd Ahmad Jami. *Divan-e Jami. Vol. I: Fatehat al-shabab, Vol. II: Wasetat al-aqd and Khatemat al-hayat.* Edited by Ala Khan Afsahzad. Tehran: Written Heritage Publication Office, Center for Iranian Studies, 1999.

Jalal al-Din Rumi, Molana. *Kolliyat-e Shams-e Tabrizi; Divan-e ghazali-yat* [The Complete Divan of Shams of Tabriz]. Intro and essay on Rumi's biography by Badiozzaman Foroozanfar. Tehran: Muasseseye, Matbuatiy-e Amir Kabir, 1958.

Kabir. "Songs of the Heart" *Poetry of Kabir.* Carlsbad, Calif.: Inner Directions Journal, The Spirit of Insight & Awakening, Spring/Summer, 2007.

Kadkani, Dr. Mohammad Reza Shafiee, editor. *Ansooy-e Harf va Sout* [Beyond Words and Sound]. From the Persian (Farsi) Literary Heritage Series: *Selected pieces from Asrarottohid (of Sheikh Abu-Saeed Abil Kheir).* 3rd Edition. Tehran: Sokhan Publications, 2009 (1388AH).

———. *Beedel Dehlavi, Sha'er-e Aieeneha [Beedel of Delhi, the Poet of Mirrors], A Study of Persian Poetry Produced in the Indian Subcontinent.* 6th Edition. Tehran: Agah Publications, 2005 (1384AH).

———. *Chesheedan-e Ta'm-e Vaqt [Savoring the Taste of Time]: Old and New Statements of Sheikh Abu-Saeed.* From the Iranian Spiritual Heritage Series, No. 3: The Mystic Heritage of Abu-Saeed Abil-Kheir, First Edition. Tehran: Sokhan Publications, 2006.

———. *Elahee-nameh* [The Book of the Beloved], by Sheikh Farideddin Attar Neyshaboori. From the Attar Collection, No. 2. Tehran: Sokhan Publications, 2006.

———. *Mateq-attair* [Conference of the Birds]. 11th Edition. From the Attar Collection, No. 1. Tehran: Sokhan Publications, 2012 (1391AH).

———. *Mokhtar-nameh* [The Book of the Sovereign, Attar's Rubais], by Sheikh Farideddin Attar Neyshaboori. First Edition. From the Attar Collection, No. 3. Tehran: Sokhan Publications, 2007.

————. *Moseebat-nameh* [The Book of Travails], by Sheikh Farideddin Attar Neyshaboori. First Edition. From the Attar Collection, No. 3. Tehran: Sokhan Publications, 2007.

————. *Neveshte-bar-darya, az miras-e erfani-e Sheikh Abol-Hasan-e Kharaqani*. [Scripture on the Sea, from Spiritual Legacy of Sheikh Abol-Hasan of Kharaqan]. Tehran: Sokhan Publications, 1988.

Kadkani, Dr. Mohammad Reza Shafiee. *Zaban-e She'r dar Nasr-e Sufieh [Poetry in Sufi Discourse, an Introduction to Elements of Style in Mystic Expression]*. From the Iranian Mystic Heritage, Meeras-e Erfanit-e Iran Series. Tehran: Sokhan Publications, 2013.

Kaseb, Azizollah, editor. *Kashkool-e Sheikh Bahai* by Bahaoddin Mohammad Abol-Samad Amoli, known as Sheikh Bahai. 9th Edition. Tehran: Goli Publications, 2007 (1385AH).

Krishnamurti, J. *Samadhi, Part 1—Maya, the Illusion of the Self*. Daniel Schmidt, writer and director. AwakenTheWorldFilm: Canada, 2017. awakentheworld.com. https://www.youtube.com/watch?v=Bw9zSMsKcwk. 2/2018.

Mansoor, Jahangeer, editor. *Divan of Attar* by Sheikh Farideddin Attar Neyshaboori. Biography by Badiozzaman Foroozanfar. 5th Edition. Tehran: Sokhan Publications, 2006.

Maharshi, Sri Ramana. *Sayings of Ramana Maharshi*. Compiled and Classified by A.R. Natajaran. Pocket Edition. Bangalore: Ramana Maharshi Centre for Learning, 1992.

Masoomi, Reza. *Arefaneha, Jami az Oqianoos-e Beekaran-e Erfan* [Selections of Mystic Poetry, a Cup from the Infinite Ocean of Gnosi]. 6th Edition. Tehran. Nashr-e Eshare Publications, 1991.

Movahhed, Mohammad Ali, editor. *Maqhalat-e Shams-e Tabrizi, Shamseddin Mohammad Tabrizi* [The Essays of Shams of Tabriz]. 3rd Edition. Tehran: Kharazmi Publications, 2006 (1385AH).

Naseri, Naser. *Jelvehaye Tanzhaye Erfani dar Asar-e Attar* [Aspects of Spiritual Humor in Attar's Works]. Member Scientific Committee Free Islamic University, Khoy Unit, article published in 2007.

Riahi, Pari. *Intellect and Reason in Rumi*. Foreword by Professor Seyyed Hosein Nasr. First Edition. Tehran: Iranian Institute of Philosophy, 2005 (1384AH).

Ritter, Helmut and John O'Kane. "The Ocean of the Soul; Men, the World and God in the Stories of Farideddin Attar" in *Handbook of Oriental Studies, Section 4: Near & Middle East* (Book 69). Boston: Brill Academic Publications, 2012.

Farsi version of the above: *Daryay-e Ja'n Vol. 1 & 2*. Translated by Abbas Zaryab Khoy-ee. Tehran: Al-hadi International Publications, 1998 (1377AH).

Shirazi, Seyyed Ahmad Beheshti, editor. *The Rubais of Khaje Abol-vafa Kharazmi, known as Pir-e Freshte (The Angelic Master)*. First Edition. Tehran: Rozaneh Publications, 2016 (1395AH).

Sogyal Rinpoche. *The Tibetan Book of Living and Dying*. San Francisco: Harper Collins, 1992.

Vafaie, Mohammad Afsheen, editor. *Resaleye Sepahsalar dar Manaqeb-e Hazrat Khodavandgar* [Sepahsalar's Essay on Rumi by Fereydoon ebn-e Ahmad Sepahsalar. Tehran: Sokhan Publications, 2006 (1385AH).

Wei, Wei Wu. *Open Secret*. Boulder, Colorado: Sentient Publications, LLC, 2004.

Wei, Wei Wu. *Why Lazarus Laughed: The Essential Doctrine of the Zen-Advaita-Tantra*. Boulder, Colorado: Sentient Publications, LLC, 2003.

Wu, John C. H. *The Golden Age of Zen, The Classic Work of the Foundation of Zen Philosophy*. With an introduction by Thomas Merton. First Edition. New York: Doubleday, 1996.

Xu Yun. *Empty Cloud, The Autobiography of the Chinese Zen Master Xu Yun*. Translated by Charles Luk (Lu K'uan Yu). Edited by Richard Hunn. Shaftsbury, Dorset, England: Element Books, 1988.

Tzu, Chuang. *Inner Chapters*. Gai-Fu Feng and Jane English, trans. New York, London: Hay House Inc., 2014.

OTHER HOHM PRESS TITLES BY VRAJE ABRAMIAN

WINDS OF GRACE
Poetry, Stories and Teachings of Sufi Mystics and Saints
Renditions by Vraje Abramian

This book gathers together extracts from biographies of both Sufi and non-Sufi sages, stories and statements about them, as well as poetry attributed to them. The translator's intention is singular: to encourage individuals on their path. Reading works about and by saints and sages reminds us of the vital need in the wayfarer's life to keep focused on the Heart, the Divine, the Beloved, amidst so many contenders for one's attention.

Paperback with French flaps, 288 pages, $24.95
ISBN: 978-1-942493-06-8

~

NOBODY SON OF NOBODY
Poems of Shaikh Abu-Saeed Abil-Kheir
Renditions by Vraje Abramian

Anyone who has found a resonance with the love-intoxicated poetry of Rumi, must read the poetry of Shaikh Abil-Kheir. This renowned, but little-known Sufi mystic of the 10th century, preceded Rumi by over two hundred years on the same path of annihilation into God. This book contains translations and poetic renderings of 195 short selections from the original Farsi, the language in which Abil-Kheir wrote.

These poems deal with the longing for union with God, the desire to know the Real from the false, the inexpressible beauty of creation when seen through the eyes of Love, and the many attitudes of heart, mind and feeling that are necessary to those who would find the Beloved, The Friend, in this life.

Paper, 120 pages, $12.95   ISBN: 978-1-890772-08-6
                                            e-book ISBN: 978-1-942493-04-0

To order, visit our website at www.hohmpress.com

OTHER HOHM PRESS TITLES BY VRAJE ABRAMIAN

THIS HEAVENLY WINE
Poems from the Divan-e Jami
Renditions by Vraje Abramian

Following in the footsteps of the Persian mystical poets Rumi, Hafez and Nizami, the timeless works in this collection express the poet's overwhelming devotion to and longing for the Divine Beloved. The author, Nooreddin Abdurrahman Ibn-e Ahmad-e Jami, referred to colloquially as Jami (Jaami) was born in eastern Khorasan, Iran in 1414 and died in 1492. Jami's poetry seethes with spiritual ardor without being sentimental. His themes are varied, but ultimately lead back to a singular teaching that the Divine is not separate from the one who seeks and loves.

Paper, 142 pages, $12.95 ISBN: 978-1-890772-56-7
e-book ISBN: 978-1-942493-02-0

～

SWEET SORROWS
Selected Poems of Sheikh Farideddin Attar Neyshaboori
Renditions by Vraje Abramian

For anyone interested in Sufism in particular, or mystical understanding in general, Attar's works are indispensable. His influence on later giants, such as the mystic poet Jalaleddin Rumi, is well documented.

Attar is mostly known in the West for his *Biographies of the Saints*, and for *Conference of the Birds*; but he has also produced a number of other masterpieces well-known among lay persons and Sufi practitioners in Iran, and in cultures influenced by the Persian language. *Sweet Sorrows* is the first compilation of Attar's lesser-known works in English. The translator, Vraje Abramian, has selected 350 short verses that cover a wide range of Attar's poetic moods—from somewhat satirical and humorous to tender and heartbreaking.

Paper, 224 pages, $17.95 ISBN: 978-1-935387-42-8
e-book ISBN: 978-1-935387-53-4

To order, visit our website at www.hohmpress.com

OTHER HOHM PRESS TITLES BY VRAJE ABRAMIAN

THE SOUL AND A LOAF OF BREAD
The Teachings of Sheikh Abol-Hasan of Kharaqan
Translation by Vraje Abramian

This book contains new translations of over 100 short statements of Sufic wisdom from Sheikh Abol-Hasan of Kharaqhan (died 1034), a "Sufis' Sufi." His near anonymity was deliberate, according to the Sheikh's wish when he lived. Despite being a hidden saint, his spiritual affinity and grace are still acknowledged among the living Sufi circles across Iran and in the region.

In this collection, Sheikh Kharaqani's statements—collected and recorded centuries ago by his companions—have been rendered into English for the international reader. To best appreciate these secrets today, readers need a longing heart, earnestly seeking for the heritage that we humans, enmeshed in the grossness of material existence, so easily forget.

Paper, 120 pages, $12.95   ISBN: 978-1-935387-12-1
                                   e-book ISBN: 978-1-942493-01-3

To order, visit our website at www.hohmpress.com

OTHER TITLES OF INTEREST FROM HOHM PRESS

RUMI ~ THIEF OF SLEEP
180 Quatrains from the Persian
Translations by Shahram Shiva
Foreword by Deepak Chopra

This book contains 180 translations of Rumi's short devotional poems, or *quatrains*. Shiva's versions are based on his own carefully documented translation from the Farsi (Persian), the language in which Rumi wrote.

"In *Thief Of Sleep*, Shahram Shiva (who embodies the culture, the wisdom and the history of Sufism in his very genes) brings us the healing experience. I recommend his book to anyone who wishes *to remember*. This book will help you do that."
—Deepak Chopra, author of *How to Know God*

Paper, 120 pages, $11.95   ISBN: 978-1-890772-05-5

~

CRAZY AS WE ARE
Selected Rubais from the Divan-I Kebir *of Mevlana Celaleddin Rumi*
Introduction and Translation by Dr. Nevit O. Ergin

This book is a collection of 128 previously untranslated *rubais*, or quatrains (four-line poems which express one complete idea), of the 13th-century scholar and mystic poet Rumi. Filled with the passion of both ecstasy and pain, Rumi's words may stir remembrance and longing, or challenge complacency in the presence of awesome love. Ergin's translations (directly from Farsi, the language in which Rumi wrote) are fresh and highly sensitive, reflecting his own resonance with the path of annihilation in the Divine as taught by the great Sufi masters.

Paper, 88 pages, $9.95   ISBN 978-0-934252-30-0
          e-book ISBN: 978-1-942493-32-7

To order, visit our website at www.hohmpress.com

OTHER TITLES OF INTEREST FROM HOHM PRESS

THE MIRROR OF THE SKY
Songs of the Bauls of Bengal
Translated by Deben Bhattacharya

Baul music today is prized by world musicologists, and Baul lyrics are treasured by readers of ecstatic and mystical poetry. Their music, lyrics and accompanying dance reflect the passion, the devotion and the iconoclastic freedom of this remarkable sect of musicians and lovers of the Divine, affectionately known as "God's troubadours."

The Mirror of the Sky is a translation of 204 songs, including an extensive introduction to the history and faith of the Bauls, and the composition of their music. It includes a CD of authentic Baul artists, recorded as much as forty years ago by Bhattacharya, a specialist in world music. The current CD is a rare presentation of this infrequently documented genre.

Paper, 288 pages, $24.95 (includes CD) ISBN: 978-0-934252-89-8
CD sold separately, $16.95   e-book ISBN: 978-1-942493-03-7

~

SONGS OF THE QAWALS OF INDIA
Islamic Lyrics of Love and God
Recordings by Deben Bhattacharya

These recordings of a centuries-old musical form were made in Kashmir and in Varanasi, India. Five exquisite songs speak of love, life and death, of God and the dedicated beings, of the Prophet Muhammad and his early followers.

Qawali in its current musical form was introduced in India towards the end of the 13th century by a great musician named Amir Khasru, whose ancestors came to India from Iran. Sung in both Hindi and Urdu-speaking regions of North India, the instruments used are those popular with the folk musicians of North India: the harmonium, the *sarangi*, the double-headed drum (*dholak*) and a pair of cymbals.

Includes photos, introduction and song lyrics
60-minute CD, $15.00   ISBN: 978-1-890772-12-3

To order, visit our website at www.hohmpress.com